I found the book you are about to
yet I find it difficult to explain what I love about it, ...,
with conviction, that from among a group of extremely strong entries,
I would pick this manuscript for publication. Like most great poetry,
Life in a Field is impossible to summarize or paraphrase. More than
most poetry, it eludes formal categorization. *Life in a Field* is hybrid,
mongrel—part allegory, part parable, part fable, part fairytale, part
futurist pastoral set in the past or an alternate reality. In this short
collection, Peterson has created her own original, heterodox form. "It's
about a girl and a donkey, but not *really* but yes *really*," I tried to
explain to anyone who would listen, when I first read the book. "The
girl is a *real* girl and the donkey is a *real* donkey, but of course they're
not *real-real* because it's *poetry* (well, prose poetry) and a donkey in a
poem is a poem-donkey . . . but in this case not just a poem-donkey be-
cause the book neither anthropomorphizes or exoticizes the donkey (or
the girl), which allows the donkey (and girl) to feel real, true, embod-
ied, actual . . . and the book is also about the economy and motherhood
and childhood, about the nature of narrative and the narrativization
of nature. It's in conversation with a French film, but it's not, for the
most part, *abstract*, or *theoretical...* and there are photographs!" Seeing
a baffled look on my listener's face, I'd switch tactics and say, simply,
"Well, I'm picking it, and I can't wait for you to read it!"

When my children were young, there were books they demanded I
read them dozens of times a day. Often these books pleased the mouth
and ear and in that way penetrated the body. Their phonemes woke
up the mouth like salt then sugar then lemon. They were songs my
children could make their own through memory; they inspired dances
they could adapt to their own small bodies. But there was another
quality that drew my children to certain books. My sons were obses-
sively drawn to books that in some way befuddled them. Sometimes
these books contained a discordance between text and illustration
or something important about the story didn't quite make sense. My
children requested, over and over, perhaps wanting to unravel a mys-
tery or master a concept but most often they seemed to love to wander
(accompanied by their mother and therefore safe) through zones of
strangeness, incomprehensibility and wonder.

Like these books, *Life in a Field* delights me in its simple, surprising, exquisite language. Like these books, *Life in a Field* bewilders me in the most captivating way. I feel, from the first pages, that I *know* the (unknowable) girl, *know* the (unknowable) donkey, that I am in a familiar albeit curious, unchartable land. I am in the land of "story," a land in which I've been lost and found and through which I've wandered for most of my life. I am bewildered or be-wild-er-ed, brought into my own body, the present, the real, and made wild with being. I can't wait for you to read it!

RACHEL ZUCKER
author of *SoundMachine*
and judge of the Omnidawn Open

Life in a Field is a propulsive, gorgeously written story that, like the best fairy tales, feels both familiar and revelatory. Peterson is a master of image delivery. In her prose we see alternate and concurrent images unfold simultaneously—a lemon is both ripe and rotten, a girl is both in love with a donkey and has decided to love no one, a friend is both emotionally luminous and incapable of crying honest tears. *Life in a Field* is a triumph of language's unique ability to show us doubleexposed ideas with deft and sparkling energy.

RITA BULLWINKEL
author of *Belly Up*

"What do you do with the story you didn't wish for?" If you are Katie Peterson and Young Suh, you make the opposite story, an enchanting poetic and visual parable about everything, but particularly about the stories we tell about citizenship, belonging, capitalism, marriage, gender, nature, imagination, animals, landscapes, and the passage of time. It stars a girl, an unnamed donkey with a star mark, and a narrator who warns us to keep our distance so we don't get in the way. Our job as readers is to acknowledge that we are transients by this American river: to pitch our tent and live in the story, not to relate to it. Devastating is too small a word for the vision of goodness and proximity these poems pursue. Their deft interrogation of empathy, privilege, and the myriad ways that "beauty makes you greedy and love repurposes your greed" builds lyricism out of narrative itself. The journey *Life in a Field* takes us on makes us strange to ourselves in the best possible ways; we stand in that field and pay attention to the price of living in time.

CHIYUMA ELLIOTT
author of *At Most* and *Vigil*

Katie Peterson's work finds a new kind of happiness, and *Life in A Field* leads you on a path that's exploratory but inevitable, tricky but sturdy, earned and enduring and cerebral and impulsive and lit bright with joy. This book is splendid. It makes me happy.

This is a really lovely book.

DANIEL HANDLER
author of *Why We Broke Up* and *Bottle Grove*

Let others try to summarize the plot of Katie Peterson's odd and compelling *Life in a Field*—I want to tell you my copy of it is rife with sunshine yellow: all the thoughts and phrases I highlighted because they hurled a bolt through me. Like: "She imagined consoling a god so scared he hid from visitors in his own house." Like: "I marry you Time, purger of fortunes, handmaiden of ruin." Like a single page empty but for the word "Happy" on it. This is a book about the nature of love, time, friendship, decay, and what storytelling is for. Here, Peterson lets her generosity of mind run free.

DANA LEVIN
author of *Banana Palace*

Katie Peterson's *Life in a Field* exists, in my mind, as a painting, or as a detail—or as two dovetailing details—in a painting (like one by Bruegel, but seen through a glass lightly) that is as long as life, and as fleeting. When you reach the end, and when you reach the beginning of wondering how, you will want to return, as I—and the pictures that passed through your mind—did, not only to the beginning, but all at once to the whole panorama.

BRANDON SHIMODA
author of *The Grave in the Wall* and *The Desert*

LIFE IN A FIELD

LIFE IN A FIELD

POEMS

KATIE PETERSON
PHOTOGRAPHS BY YOUNG SUH

OMNIDAWN PUBLISHING
OAKLAND, CALIFORNIA
2021

Cover and interior photos by Young Suh

Typeset in TT Marxiana

Cover and interior design by adam b. bohannon

Library of Congress Cataloging-in-Publication Data

Names: Peterson, Katie, 1974- author.
Title: Life in a field : poems / Katie Peterson ; photographs by Young Suh.

Description: Oakland, California : Omnidawn, 2021. | Summary: "Life in a
    Field is a comedy set inside our changing climate. In the story, a girl
    and a donkey become friends, and then, decide to marry time. A lyric
    fable, Life in a Field intersperses slow-moving, cinematic paragraphs in
    image-driven, sensual prose with three folios of images by the
    photographer Young Suh. Introspection, wish, dream, and memory take on
    the character of events. A narrative voice speaks from a distance, but
    does so with candor, attempting to find a path through our daily and
    familiar strife, towards what remains of beauty and pleasure. In clear,
    exacting sentences, Life in a Field attempts, against all evidence, to
    reverse our accelerating destruction of the natural world, reminding us
    of "the cold clarity we need to continue on this earth.""-- Provided by
    publisher.
Identifiers: LCCN 2021002386 | ISBN 9781632430908 (paperback)
Subjects: LCGFT: Poetry.
Classification: LCC PS3616.E8429 L54 2021 | DDC 811/.6--dc23
LC record available at https://lccn.loc.gov/2021002386

Published by Omnidawn Publishing, Oakland, California
www.omnidawn.com   (510) 237-5472
10 9 8 7 6 5 4 3 2 1
ISBN: 978-1-63243-090-8

for Violet and Brighde, for animals and girls

Everyone who sees this film will be absolutely astonished . . .
because this film is really the world in an hour and a half.

Jean Luc Goddard
on *Au Hasard Balthazar*

Contents

PART
ONE

In this story there is a girl and there is a donkey. The girl approaches the donkey because the girl has something to say. What is it?

At first, everything had the structure of a blessing. People kept giving the girl what she needed. At the bend in the path, a river with clear water. A beautiful education. An inn at sunset. A spectacular blueberry pie in a perfect circle with a crust so flaky that the last sunlight filled its layers, which had been gently separated by the fork delaying the conclusion of the slice.

The girl found the field earlier than other girls. She didn't want to stay home. She didn't want to stay home, but it wasn't because of a discord there. Everything had been provided. A roof, an apron, a brother, a sister, a dress at Easter trimmed in eyelet with daises on the false placket and a white satin sash tied into a loose bow that did not constrict. She grew up wanting nothing. What was there to want? She wanted the sweet rolls in December to have a cross of lemon frosting, and this was not allowed. But at least she grew up wanting nothing to change. She had one brother and one sister. That was enough, yes? To have another would be to repeat, and she already lived as a repetition of a sister.

The house got bigger because the economy got better. And then, she wanted things to be as they had been. She wanted to share a room with her sister again. When they watched the spider climb across the wall, it was a movie if they were together. When she watched it alone, she terrified herself considering its mind and intentions.

The donkey's mother carried him for a year in her belly while she did the usual labors. What else she carried has not been recorded, but can be guessed— fabrics, milled flour, root vegetables, other vegetables in the right season. Always sugar carried back from the market. She forgot she had him with her most of that time. Sometimes she felt him adjusting the fold of his leg inside her, but she believed he was the movement of undigested straw. When this happened, she waited for him to move through her, like the crowds at the market waited, if she moved through them, since she might have something on her back they wanted to buy.

He was born in a good barn after a fine harvest and when he came out, the straw felt warm and smelled clean, though this second fact escaped him, enraptured as he was by the smell of his mother.

There was no childhood for the donkey, but he was brought up. They brought him to his feet, on the first and the second day, and on the third day he stood by himself. He was made for labor. The people were just trying to help. They wanted him to be himself faster. No one thought of it as an education. It seemed more like a tough regime of nutrition, or a training for a human occupation like toll taker, an occupation where what you do might never change until you are made obsolete. But there must have been a first time he stood, in the straw, just for his mother, before the farmers got involved, before the hands got greedy for their time, before they took her away for the ten day interval of her ovulation and her opportunity to breed again.

Maybe it wasn't a narrative at all. Maybe it was a sequence or a constellation. I think the storyline came after the fact. The lines were drawn through the facts after the facts happened. At the beginning of what is now England, in that dark part of history, humans learned certain abilities, for example, literacy, for example the ability to make pottery on the wheel, and lost them when violence between tribes overtook the skeleton of the Roman system. They used cups and bowls made on home soil for hundreds of years, not knowing how they had been made.

School, for the girl, made sense. One teacher told her about color, reflecting on the spectrum as if it were a series of sainted mortals. One teacher trained her hand to make its script legible, and also to know how to make what was illegible in the spirit understandable to itself, to write an angry letter, to compose a love letter. What the girl did on the page predicted a difficult freedom. One teacher helped her line up the numbers in columns that displayed their patterns of addition and subtraction. The next year the same teacher taught her division. Then multiplication came naturally, like a form of hunger. One teacher showed her Mesopotamia, and so she knew where language came from, and another showed her Africa, so she knew where the first human stood up. So what if they sometimes lost their tempers, so what if the one day that she was sick with hay fever was the day they showed a four hour long movie about Kilauea, the volcano, beautiful in destruction, the lava making the houses and villages surrender to new roads, first in liquid and then, hardened into shapes its original spew and fire could never have made.

The very best teacher left the classroom abruptly for the mountains after the year turned. The class moved on from sentences to paragraphs. The next year, the girl got a postcard of that teacher and a donkey, packing their way through the Sango de Christos, and she asked her mother if they could go visit, even though she could tell it was warmer and more dry there than any place she'd ever been. Instead, her mother helped her send a letter, and let her choose the stamp with its hothouse flower.

The heat from the girl's mouth, it's milligram of moisture, a lip-administered mistral that comes after each word, lifts the white hairs on the donkey's left ear, the only visible part of him traceable to a recessive gene. But what is she saying?

There is another way of looking at the story. Each stage on the journey was a blessing, and each blessing was a toll.

In a fairy tale, a toll can be extracted anywhere, but bridges and ferries are favored as points of service because they so clearly literalize the emotional suspension involved in a journey. The story requires the collection of the coin (the story, not the person living the story, not the troll or ferryman) and always requires that before the passage has been accomplished. The existence of the toll assures the one who pays: you will know that you had an experience.

The toll proves that the mind is very powerful. It represents the story's fear that you might go through the experience unscathed, that the world would not be enough to remind you of itself. The toll, lightened from your pocket, weighs on you, like the sun moving into place in the café just as the argument between the not-yet-married couple begins.

Have you ever noticed that only one letter divides them, toll and troll?

You are paying your attention.

And yet, a mandatory mismatch accompanies the part of the story where one has to pay. Why does a traveler in a fairy tale rarely have the money to pay a toll? Indeed, it doesn't occur to most, until you're actually at the bridge that a troll might even be there, let alone that he might possess the structure (and is the implication that the troll owns the bridge? It is hard to be sure). The reduction to barter in this case becomes comical for the story but not for the traveler. "You will give me all the ham you have, and I will allow you to cross my bridge." But the mind lags a bit behind—who says it was your bridge? No one told me about you. I have no ham.

The deal made in this instance, the deal you make agreeing to pay a toll—yes, it's funny but it's usually a deceit of a kind, a debt you'll never pay, or a debt you'll spend your life trying to get out of paying—two years of your life, your soul, your first-born. Who really gives these things away? You go on, as they say, about your business, because it's not like language takes anything from you. Especially a troll's garbled and anonymous speech. It's not like language takes anything from you immediately.

The toll, however you pay it, says, *it will not be like this forever. It will be like this a little while longer.*

It is true that everyone lives in a story. Once, I had a friend I'll call Titania. One night, I went to meet her and she had glitter on her eyes. With her, it was always a willing transformation—she followed a band for years, the concerts, the bootlegs, the fans. She married men who were open, but shut down when they weren't drunk. When her hair streaked gray in the early years of middle age it looked like a blessing from the moon. When she cried, I did not believe her. When she laughed, like the time she pointed out the young girl dancing with a man three times her age, she turned the story from something dangerous into a funny cosmology. When I met her for a drink, she had three. When I met her for a drink, I had to physically quash—I mean stay my own hand at the shop reaching for my wallet—a desire to bring her roses.

The girl is not a pretty brunette. Her hair has been bleached blonde because she likes to swim. She swims downstream from the bridge where the boys (and to be fair, their sisters) catch the small fish almost too hard to catch, so small, now, that the runoff from the mountains has been cut in half. Do you want to know if she swims naked? Yes she swims naked. Do you want to know if there is a danger she could be seen? Yes she could be seen. What is the harm in it? There has never been any harm.

The donkey grew up and became himself without his mother. It was not painful. He barely thought of her. But when he saw her, harnessed up to the market cart, his body stood at a form of attention more devoted than rigid and his eyes blinked more slowly, and whatever they had been making him do, he would not do any more, for a minute or two. Usually his mother found her way out of the picture quickly enough that her son had neither to be beaten nor scolded for looking at her beauty, something his owner would have called "wasting time" in this instance unless a lesson regarding getting from one point to another had been extracted.

In the last scene of the sad movie, the filmmaker allows the sheep to drift around the dead donkey. The camera doesn't try to follow them. When you work with animals, they are always moving out of the picture.

PART TWO

The donkey never knew the difference between a game and labor, but he knew he could get bored. And he did, pulling a rope between his teeth in a kind of race. But it wasn't a race, there wasn't another donkey! And the part of the field they had him in, closed off on all sides by fences, didn't make sense for racing—in a race it seemed you should be able to go as fast as you like, as far as you had to. In this game, the object was to cover the same track again and again with the plow, and at the end of the row, sometimes as a kindness, never really as payment, because they were good to him, they gave him a drink of water before they turned him around.

The hair inside the donkey's ear was white as new snow, though often dirty, and rarely noticed. The girl spoke into his ear in her gentlest voice. Some donkeys have what's called a star mark, an almost exact bisection of the back crossed with a vector at the neck the fades as it descends on either side of the flank. They call them Jerusalem donkeys and they are prized.

The first time the girl thought about ugliness, it was because of the still life on her mother's table. By "still life," I mean the kind of arrangement that simply happens over the course of time, based on consumption, ripeness, and what the members of the household do or don't like the task of preparing, oranges requiring a second step, peeling, in order to be eaten, and stone fruits often asking for you to discern whether to remove their rinds or just take a bite. In this instance, an eggplant rested on top of an onion, with three lemons from the backyard in the bottom of the bowl, and one lemon with a slice cut out for a glass of water after a day's work. Also, a string bag with four avocados, and two store bought lemons of a lighter color than the others balancing between that bag and the eggplant. But in the midst of all of these, one of the lemons from the yard (she knew this because it was smaller and may have even started out a bit ruined) had turned a (grotesque or angelic?) shade of silver-gray, and turned wrinkled, its rind having become an elderly skin, with the feeling of cling rather than drag, hang rather than fall. She did not move it, having an instinct for recognizing a sense of belonging that she found impossible to override, and as she grew up, she would continue to find difficult. Why move what seems so placed? If what's rotten has a place, why move it?

HEARD IN CHURCH

Since Jesus is my portion
He's a battle axe
His eye is on the sparrow
Didn't it rain

Down by the riverside
What a friend we have
Maybe someone's trying
To tell you something

Man who rode the donkey
Greatest cowboy of them all
You'll never walk alone
I'll fly away

THE DONKEY'S MOTHER'S SONG, A CAPELLA

You went and got a baby from the earth. You stuffed it up inside yourself and didn't know what it was worth. It was made of dirt. It sang a bloat, a blather, a goat-like air. You didn't want a goat so you felt stuck. Sure, sure, the barbs of wire on the fence sang, it was a goat. You forgot your intuition and you called that *thought*. You practiced goat sounds when you gave up. You ate and ate until it came out. Your fear eaten by your need. You covered it and made it warm. It was not a goat. It was a life. You walked away so it could learn to walk.

The difference between poetry and its opposite is the difference between sadness and astonishment.

The difference between poetry and astonishment is the difference between sadness and its opposite.

The difference between a sad event and an astonished person has something to do with citizenship.

The story, invested in a return, stays interested in what comes back. If you lose something, for example if you lose a baby, you might wish for another. But if you lose another baby after that, and this time you are farther along, there are two different paths the mind might take. The first is to wish for one more baby, one that will stay and be healthy. This baby would continue the story's original intent, its life, its teething would feel like a fulfillment, a word that has the word "fill" in it, the ear reminds you after you say it. The second path —well, it's not a path, it's a person—the second person wishes for two babies, because now two are owed him or her. It doesn't have to be babies. A poet writes, *I lost two cities, lovely ones.* There could be no end to this. Two is not the last number. Two is more like the possibility of any greater number. What the story might wish for could become unwieldy. And difficult to distinguish from a desire for reward.

The girl has shifted her position. She's trying not to scare the donkey. She's trying to get closer to the tuft of white inside his ear. Has she put her arms around him already, and is this actually a friendly denouement? Or has their alliance not been secured yet, and does this dance still dovetail with courtship? It seems he receives her words first as warmth, then as breath and sweat. I suspect that, if we get closer, our presence will startle each of them in opposite directions and the point is to keep their combination in the landscape, isn't it? So we should stay here.

Of his occasional glimpses of his mother, the donkey makes a story. The time between, like a piece of cloth cut: after the moment of measuring the scissors equals a kind of surprise. Surprise is the story. No order embeds itself in his story like a reporter who will show you the way to the bunker or up the ladder to the place the bombs are.

The story cannot predict anything for the donkey, poor creature. He knows neither the hour nor the day. But the world calendars the sudden gestures it makes towards him—market day, the day the owner delivers flour and money to the banker to address the possibility of foreclosure twice a year, picnic day when the donkey's mother takes the children of the other farmer down to the river to play.

How can he be sad? He is a donkey. He accommodates, based on resources. He goes where the food is. The story he lives through includes sudden changes of world. It does not necessarily mean plot. It does not mean your expectations are fulfilled. Are the donkey's expectations fulfilled? The donkey is often scared. The story marks the moment that one version of the story makes the idea of "the only story" obsolete. It obsolesces that. I am so glad there is a verb with a direct object to describe what it does.

And the world of the barn has its comforts. Though a goat can be selfish, the barn's stalls are separated so that each animal can eat all the food he or she wants, alone, and isn't that the best case scenario? Both privacy and abundance?

And there is not another donkey and isn't this also good, not to have to compete? To be the only one of your kind? Isn't this what everyone wants?

In less prosperous countries, they say, the isolation of the donkey is a problem. Most families can only afford one, and they treat it badly. But here, the solitude of the well cared for animal is a point of pride and can be carried like a banner.

A donkey doesn't *realize*—he eats.

Who comes here, to this field, this gorgeous expanse, in search of something he cannot name—not wealth, but a fortune of the spirit, a freshness denied him in the cities? The valley glitters and brightens in the morning before its light becomes simply a condition of being. At night, the land grows dark, and the houses, lit from within, appear to be hoarding whatever has no relationship with scarcity. And then, the sun rises again.

When the girl moves closer, the donkey doesn't move back, but stiffens a little, quails inside, and the outside is the afterbirth of his nervousness, a useless trembling in place that could be useful if he knew what to do with it. What did she say to him?

Breathe body your chances are not exhaustive if you walk by the river you'll see the transients in their leisure questioning the rudiments of the social structure. The wages of sin are sunlight and sleep. Dreams are healthcare in this landscape. They're national.

As the animal grows into work, the human grows into love. The summer the girl's hips widened, her breasts began to require confinement. Through the hints and guesses of another girl she knew what to do, but she could have used a better teacher, someone with the best interests of the language at heart. Maybe so many women teach because they all could have used better teachers.

For the girl, the plot is the orchard. The abundance of this particular landscape in her blood, she does not remember a time when the harvest didn't brighten the yard she was born in sight of. The summer came with ease, like a monarch taking its due. But even the best harvest yields when it gets picked to scarcity, even when that picking is appropriate, mandated, even when all is right with the gleaning. I say it was the perfect time. I say you would have said so too, but even then, the fall brought rains and the winter brought the skeletons her likeness-making mind would make of the natural world. Even then, the girl accommodated scarcity. The plot relies on the splitting of the second here. The plot requires you to recognize the split inside the second when one believes, really believes, that no spring can overtake the world again. That sadness. The plot insists on this lie, the tiny crack in the best possible world that turns a wish into its opposite, that turns a desire for rebirth into a desire for escape.

Because we are so far past this story, I wish to linger on it. This story is not your story. You are not meant to relate to it. You are meant to pitch a tent inside this page like a down and out person might do by the American River, under the trestle tracks, where the overgrowth and heat and greenery and shade in proximity to water makes a drought as unlikely as a marriage of equals in a century where women can't read. You are meant to believe you can live here.

The girl said, "it's time." I could see her two lips forming the "t" with the teeth underneath, at least I could see the unlikely opening after that pointed sound. Or did she say "tame?"

THE GIRL'S MOTHER'S SONG,
A CAPPELLA

How lovely the days when the girl's not a body. Yet, yet, when
the girl's not a shape, just a shape of a person, not the nape of
her neck shining white, not an Adam's Apple and evidence of
a trachea, but evidence of breath, not a breathing with breasts,
just a breath in the belly, a breath in me.

Anything wild wasn't allowed for a landscape for the girl's play without her safe accompaniment by her mother. But with her mother's accompaniment, all was allowed. They went walking or on bikes to the field where the list of species she could identify grew by the day, assisted by books, and the list of species she could identify grew to include rapacious names like lupine, wolf's beard, wolf's bane. But they were just names. There was no harm. She was accompanied. She did not go alone, though one time she stood in the child-high mustard just to breathe there, and she hid where it grew dense and thick and stayed until she was called.

But it was only a matter of time. She went alone, crossed the bridge into the field. And nothing happened. She stood there. It was a public field, in the sense that no one remembered who owned it. There isn't anything like this anymore. An extra field. She just stood in the quiet. There was no household. And then she went home.

No water under the bridge. A dry season. She went home. She wasn't even late. She hadn't lost a shoe or her father's mother's bracelet with the golden chain attaching its pieces together in addition to the clasp. She had no sunburn, no earned thirst. In no way had she gotten lost.

But the girl's absence from her mother's sight initiated a worry her mother couldn't drop, like a petal-stripped flower held onto out of guilt. It was not late. The mother wasn't even making dinner. "Where have you been?"

The girl, standing in her own yard, knew the answer. She had to lie. To say she knew she had to lie is to misspeak. She lied as immediately as a donkey drinks water. She spoke with her whole mouth. "In the corner of our yard, safe behind the trees."

It was on that day or possibly the next she saw clearly that she would never tell her mother everything that happened to her. Her left hand clutched a piece of lupine, its tiny broom, which she placed inside a storybook about a raven queen who wished to marry a human rather than between the pages of the flower press with four screws her mother had given her.

Falsehoods bring anxiety and truth makes people calm. One must ask first in any situation who is anxious and who is telling the truth.

When the girl went to the field again, she saw the donkey.

PART
THREE

How can you tell a donkey is unhappy? You can tell a donkey is unhappy because the animal exhibits stereotypical behaviors. The short list of these behaviors includes pacing in an approximate figure eight and repeating a high pitched bray, even with a mouth full of hay. The long list includes shimmying the neck into any space of an available body. Each moment of a story is like that, a mistake made into a behavior. What if a story can only be the opposite of what actually happened? Each thing you don't trust from your actual memory becomes a moment worth telling. One poet calls each word of a poem "a step away from chance." I have always thought that the opposite of chance was focus.

And so, a beautiful scene gets bought by such disquiet, the having to do the same thing each day and never being paid. What would a donkey do with wages?

You don't need to be running from anywhere but home to be a criminal. You don't need to be running from anywhere but home To be a criminal, you don't need to run anywhere.

Like lots of girls, she thought about running away. Rucksack made of hobo handkerchief tied to a stick. One change of clothes, a pack of matches, a few tins of sardines, then off. The open road. Bedtime whenever she wanted it to be. In another version, the big city. Her name in lights, she'd make it, she'd show them all. But to tell oneself this story you must deny reality. You must believe the road is not dangerous, or invent, in the city, a safe house for girls. Still, when the girl dreamed of running away it was the guilt that kept her from doing it, not the logistics. The long faces of her parents. Her mother's face floating ghostly on the other side of the window, the one with the planter box of geraniums framing her family kitchen. How unfair. Denying reality is a privilege of the imagination, like the right to freely assemble. Like the right to vote. Everyone deserves it.

There was a church in the village where the girl and the donkey lived. The donkey didn't actually live *in the village,* he lived *on a farm outside the village* but he counted. She counted even though she wasn't quite grown because her parents counted her. Why did he count? There was a church. It shone white on a sunny day. On a rainy day, it occurred to the landscape as a refuge. When the girl went with her mother for the Sunday service she felt nothing. When she went by herself at empty times like Tuesdays, she didn't know what she felt but she called it loneliness. She imagined consoling a god so scared he hid from visitors in his own house.

She didn't feel much, but that wasn't sad. What she felt didn't hurt her. It didn't sit upon her like a child on the chest of a father picnicking in the grass. It didn't *weigh.* It just was. The light came in through the windows on either side of the cross, which, without a body, looked just like another window, without the glass. Inside, it looked like the worshippers were worshipping the reoriented crossbeams of an early stage of a house.

She didn't dislike money, but she couldn't hold on to it. She couldn't breathe when she held it. Her palms sweat in excess and the money slipped out.

As for the donkey—it was not that he knew how to wait for the girl, it was simply that he had nowhere else to go. In the sad movie that is the opposite of the story you are reading, the baker's son is cruel to the girl and the donkey. He is cruel to the girl before he is ever cruel about the donkey, but he becomes more cruel to the donkey because of the girl. What do you do with the story you didn't wish for?

She preferred to stand in the field. It had no purpose. It was just something she wanted to do. The weather grew more violent over the years of her life but she was always all right. She never didn't have a shelter to return to. She could leave the field when she wished and go inside.

One incarnation of daily light I have never been able to save in words backgrounds the memory of my first trip to a particular oral surgeon, the man who would remove my wisdom teeth weeks later, under general anesthetic, which was not necessary, but an insistent recommendation of my hyperbolic mother. A precise, rather than vague, dappling makes invisible trees take shape against a fence, or a wall, usually in the late hours of the morning when anything fresh has become impossible. This light marries waiting and death, and I do not wish for it, but, when it arrives, as it did a few minutes ago, I feel a strange familiarity, and my tongue traces the inside of my mouth.

In that place, at that time, was no shortage of fields. They sur-
rounded the town. Insulated it, like snow would have done, if
the town had grown in a snowy place. The fields were not pub-
lic spaces exactly but sort of. You had to trespass but everyone
did it. You had to trespass but the lines were unclear. You had
to trespass but to be caught did not even mean a reprimand.
If anything, it meant being offered a drink of water. Of course,
generosity might have its own consequences.

Ownership doesn't determine everything, says the bright sun
shining on the star-mark that crosses the back of the donkey.

The girl knew if she put her arms out, the donkey would not know what to do with them.

The girl's voice enters the donkey, not her tongue. Civilization should take a page from this. Each and every last man should take a page from this. And she does not sing and her breasts are not outlined by her light summer dress. She's wearing a mechanic's jumpsuit with her name stitched on it in script. She's not wearing a black lace brasserie underneath. Everything she has, she's been given by her mother. Her town might be the last one without a store but the other towns aren't telling. Clothes in her town are like flowers in a tropical country, everyone gets enough, no one wants too many, because they're always around, always there, really, a top hat on a haystack, a lace petticoat draped over a fence, a t shirt from a National Park found at the edge of the forest. The firefighters in her town are never overworked until the end of the season.

I wanted to let go of sugar and eat everything else. I estranged myself from bread. Enough eating Christmas for this blood-stream. Enough celebration for this liver. Enough appetite. I looked for something else. I would have done anything. This is the nature of a bargain. You would do anything, and then you are asked to do a specific thing you do not wish to do. This is the difference between me and the donkey, whose opposite I am. The donkey doesn't want to do anything but eat.

She's saying, "no work" or is it, "no worst?" Is she quoting or, saying something like a prophecy? When she makes the words with her mouth, her eyes light up. And the donkey exhibits stereotypical behavior and she believes she experiences love, or at least, the aftermath of beauty, which is love's opposite. Opposite, because beauty makes you greedy and love repurposes your greed as selflessness.

They cannot even go for a walk together. A walk together doesn't even make sense. She can read to him but he won't read back. But maybe for the donkey, memory is a form of reading. When she touches his neck he remembers that another good person did so. He puts together then, with his imagination, *a la* Ignatius Loyola, the original scene of goodness. The original scene of goodness is a person taking mercy on a donkey as his mother was led away to another field. A human who knew enough to say *sorry,* and maybe draw his or her hand along the neck to indicate to the young donkey, a child, that warmness still existed in the world.

The original scene of goodness involves a stranger.

The original scene of goodness isn't a family.

Money isn't hidden from the original scene of goodness, but there's also another currency.

Years after the scene in question, someone with only her best interests at heart, someone so skilled in language that she made her living that way, someone with an office in the trees, someone with a sunny disposition still capable of enduring cold weather, asked the girl, *when you were little, what kind of a man did you think you were going to marry?* And she said, *I never thought of that. I never thought of that*, the girl turns and says, years later, after womanhood has asserted itself in her. It's as if she's saying, *I was too busy with the donkey.*

Since the girl and the donkey are friends, they must have examined each other. They must have seen each other's bodies. Their differences when they examined each other, however, went unexplored. Rain, snow, the curses of the old, the laughter of the young: the world went on because a current of love secretly makes the world go on. Picnic in the one dry spot on the wet field. Point out the flowers to each other. Deny the existence of anything other than a perfect summer.

The donkey baby had no name. Once born, he had less than that, a name bestowed out of just enough care. A name must worry in excess about its own appropriateness in order to truly count. To name someone himself, to "donkey" a donkey has an apt simplicity but isn't anything really.

On the other hand, to name a girl means a girl must appear. For instance, if you were to name a girl *Francesca Joy*. If that was the name you might choose. You might imagine lace in her future, but you wouldn't doubt her nerve. If you were to name her *Emily*, you might imagine the lace to take a more geometric shape. In any scene on the beach, *Emily* would run. To go back to *Francesca Joy* for a minute, you might doubt she was a runner. So let us name her *Emily* instead, and maybe the joy can be implied. Let us not gild the lily. Our first try tried too hard. Our second try has given birth to something small. Now we must try again. What does the "other hand" look like? Is it a left hand? Why does it always come in to remind you of the way things don't have to happen? Is there a way things don't have to happen?

After all, what is a girl if no young man appears?

Happy

PART
FOUR

In this story, there is a girl and there is a donkey. What good friends they are, and they began as strangers! He has taught her everything she needs to know about happiness. She has fed him handfuls of hay until he was almost satisfied. They have gainsaid the horizon together. They have decided not to run away. What do they do, now that they have reached this point? And what about us? What do we do about them?

It is right to pause on the word "friend." There exists no other word we use with such a civilized agreement not to know what it means. In this respect, friendship resembles government.

This isn't a love story. This story intends to refute the creation of the world.

Language is tricky. As it says in the Bible, *I appeal to you on the basis of faith in things not seen.*

But then again, pictures swim in our heads.

The girl and the donkey have a similarity. They have decided to marry time.

Each in their own way.

I marry you time in the name of the farther and the sun and what's only lost

says the girl.

I marry you in the name of the bother and the fun and these lonely fears

says the donkey.

They are veiled in civilization.

I have seen over one hundred human weddings and not one of them has lacked the feeling of forestalling something. Even though a church keeps the weather outside. I saw a bride with impacted wisdom teeth walk down the aisle to a waiting ambulance, pausing at her groom.

The flowers at a donkey wedding are never for looking at—what a waste of flowers! Beauty means to eat. To other donkeys, his speech sounds sweet, he has been well fed, he has fallen asleep with flowers in his mouth.

I have heard they perform actual weddings between donkeys in India, in Turkey, to forestall disaster, to prevent or provoke a particular weather event.

The flowers at a human wedding cause great trauma. Anyone with sense doubles the price. You must be careful to not even whisper the cause of your purchase to a florist. Don't even think it in their presence. You'd be better off going to the grocery and buying roses at the top of your lungs.

Everyone has to marry eventually, says the 19th century, says capital, says the tax-free rich. Says the judge, everyone must handcuff themselves to love.

But how long can they stand in the field like that, her arms around his neck? Her ear looking for his heart? He will get restless and uncomfortable. She will become tired of this gesture. Time will once again turn our interpretation of their pose—this flirtation with the ridiculous, converted into pity—into impatience and a bad smell. Her ear will sweat.

But for now let them have it.

Let civilization have the original scene of goodness.

The story frozen in place before it has to *happen*.

But in this version the girl speaks.

The sky is falling, she says to him. Just yesterday I saw a piece of it hit the lake on the far side of town and land in the form of a cloud. The ground seizes up in drought. Just yesterday I saw cracks in the earth. Yesterday, brushfires followed by downpours, then immediate flooding. All the more reason to talk about flowers. I will place bunches of them around your bridle. I will weave them through your harness. They will not constrain you. I will make a bouquet of many colors for you to eat.

Time I will marry you says the girl though you have asked me roughly and not even bought me a ring. Time I marry you to-day though the minister is lacking and the church has shut its doors on us because I am not approved of, I have been disobe-dient, I crossed the field without permission. I went into the church and felt nothing and did not even try harder to believe what I was told, intuition being richer, intuition being bridal, waiting on nothing but its own readiness.

Time I will marry you though you do not respect my body. All you have given me, muscle and bone, hair and skin, you have taken away and replaced with like matter of a lesser duration. You have taken my story again and again. You have reached inside me and taken my best parts and I marry you, marry you.

The girl does not think. Pictures pass through her mind. They associate freely, which means, in an order she has yet to dis-cern.

The donkey brays. He kneels in the field. The image so radiant it reinvents religion as an accident.

I marry you Time, purger of fortunes, handmaiden of ruin, enemy of mothers, unwilling melter of the glaciers that surround us, as we sleep, with the cold clarity we need to continue on this earth.

Debts

Bertha and her mother, Elizabeth Bishop, Betsy Bogue,
Robert Bresson, Mary Calabrese, Emily Dickinson, Chiyuma
Elliott, Louise Gluck, Meera Heller, Ezekiel Reffe Hogan,
Walt Hunter, Gerard Manley Hopkins, Amelia Klein, Chris
Marker, Stephane Mallarme, Michael C. Peterson, Paul the
Apostle, Margaret Ronda, William Shakespeare, Antonin
Scalia, Keith Wollenberg

Gratitude

I thank the American Academy of Arts and Letters, the
Chancellor's Fund at UC Davis, and the Mills College
Museum of Art for giving life to this project in the form of
time and money. Special thanks to Stephanie Hanor at Mills
for nurturing the work that inspired this book, and all of
the donkeys who worked on the show, "Can We Live Here?
Stories from a Difficult World."

KATIE PETERSON is the author of four previous
collections of poetry, including *A Piece of Good News*. She
has published poetry in *The Journal of Alta California*,
Literary Imagination, *Poetry Northwest* and other magazines.
Her third collection, *The Accounts*, won the Rilke Prize
from the University of North Texas. She is Professor and
Chancellor's Fellow at the University of California at Davis,
where she directs the M.F.A. program in Creative Writing.
She lives in Berkeley with her husband, Young Suh, and
their daughter Emily.

Life in a Field
Katie Peterson

Cover and interior photos by Young Suh

Cover and interior typefaces: TT Marxiana

Cover and interior design by adam b. bohannon

Printed in the United States
by Books International, Dulles, Virginia
On 55# Glatfelter B19 Antique
Acid Free Archival Quality Recycled Paper

Publication of this book was made possible in part by gifts from
Katherine & John Gravendyk in honor of Hillary Gravendyk,
Francesca Bell, Mary Mackey, and The New Place Fund

Omnidawn Publishing
Oakland, California
Staff and Volunteers, Spring 2021

Rusty Morrison & Ken Keegan, senior editors & co-publishers
Kayla Ellenbecker, production editor & poetry editor
Gillian Olivia Blythe Hamel, senior editor & book designer
Trisha Peck, senior editor & book designer
Rob Hendricks, Omniverse editor, marketing editor & post-pub editor
Cassandra Smith, poetry editor & book designer
Sharon Zetter, poetry editor & book designer
Liza Flum, poetry editor
Matthew Bowie, poetry editor
Jason Bayani, poetry editor
Anthony Cody, poetry editor
Juliana Paslay, fiction editor
Gail Aronson, fiction editor
Izabella Santana, fiction editor & marketing assistant
Laura Joakimson, marketing assistant specializing in Instagram & Facebook
Ashley Pattison-Scott, executive assistant & Omniverse writer
Ariana Nevarez, marketing assistant & Omniveres writer